The Many Accomplishments of *Elijah McCoy*

African-American Inventor Grade 5 | Children's Biographies

DISSECTED LIVES
auto biographies

First Edition, 2021

Published in the United States by Speedy Publishing LLC, 40 E Main Street, Newark, Delaware 19711 USA.

© 2021 Baby Professor Books, an imprint of Speedy Publishing LLC

Baby Professor Books are available at special discounts when purchased in bulk for industrial and sales-promotional use. For details contact our Special Sales Team at Speedy Publishing LLC, 40 E Main Street, Newark, Delaware 19711 USA. Telephone (888) 248-4521 Fax: (210) 519-4043.

10 9 8 7 6 * 5 4 3 2 1

Print Edition: 9781541960886
Digital Edition: 9781541963887
Hardcover Edition: 9781541973268

See the world in pictures. Build your knowledge in style.
www.speedypublishing.com

Table of Contents

CHAPTER ONE:
The Birth, Early Years and
Personal Life of Elijah McCoy 7

CHAPTER TWO:
The Inventions of Elijah McCoy 33

CHAPTER THREE:
The Death and Legacy of Elijah McCoy 61

ELIJAH MCCOY

Do you ever watch television? Do you go online? Have you ever taken a bus or a train? Many people can answer yes to these questions. Do you ever stop to think of what life was like without them? Do you ever wonder how these things came to be?

All these things are possible because someone or some people came up with them. This book will focus on a man who invented many things. His name is Elijah McCoy. The book will talk about his birth, early years, and personal life. Then, it will talk about some of his most well-known inventions. The book will end with his death and legacy.

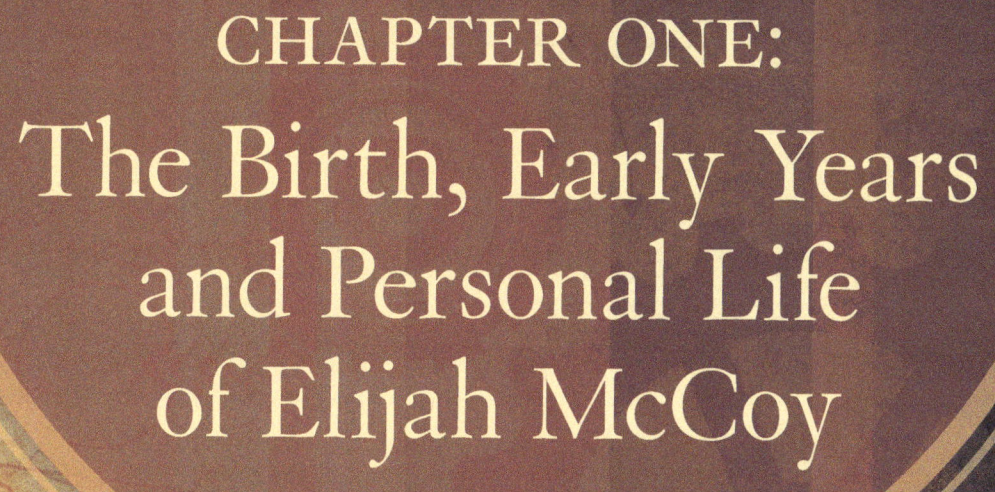

CHAPTER ONE:
The Birth, Early Years and Personal Life of Elijah McCoy

Elijah McCoy was born in what today is the country of Canada. At the time, it was a colony of Britain. The colony was divided into two areas: Upper Canada and Lower Canada. Upper Canada was where most of the English speakers lived. Lower Canada was where most of the French speakers lived.

MAP OF UPPER AND LOWER CANADA.

PARK HOUSE IN COLCHESTER SOUTH IN ONTARIO WAS A REFUGE FOR THOSE ESCAPING SLAVERY IN THE 1800S.

McCoy was born in Upper Canada. It was in a place known as Colchester Township. This was in what is now the province of Ontario. The year was around 1843. His father was George McCoy. His mother was Mildred Goins.

ELIJAH'S PARENTS WERE SLAVES AND THEIR ANCESTORS HAD BEEN FORCED INTO SLAVERY.

George McCoy and Mildred Goins McCoy used to live in Kentucky. They were slaves there. Their ancestors had been forced into slavery. They were brought to the United States from Africa.

Both George and Mildred decided to flee to Upper Canada to escape slavery. They did so by using the Underground Railroad. This was in 1837.

GEORGE AND MILDRED FLED TO UPPER CANADA TO ESCAPE SLAVERY USING THE UNDERGROUND RAILROAD.

Did you know?

The Underground Railroad was the name of a secret system. The system was used to help smuggle runaway slaves to freedom. Slaves would be helped to move secretly from one location to another. Many moved from southern states to northern states. Others went all the way to Canada. Estimates of between 40,000 and 100,000 people were helped to find freedom.

THE UNDERGROUND RAILROAD WAS THE NAME
OF A SECRET SYSTEM THAT WAS USED TO HELP
SMUGGLE RUNAWAY SLAVES TO FREEDOM.

After arriving in Upper Canada, George McCoy did military duty for a short period. Following his military service, he received one hundred and sixty acres of farmland. It was on this land that his son, Elijah McCoy, was born. Young Elijah would spend all his childhood being raised there.

GEORGE MCCOY DID MILITARY DUTY FOR A SHORT PERIOD.

ELIJAH DEVELOPED A KEEN INTEREST IN HOW MACHINES WORKED.

When Elijah was a boy in school, one of the things that he studied was machinery. He soon developed a keen interest in how machines worked. He liked to learn how they operated. He was fascinated by tools and devices. This would later lead to his career choices. It would also lead to many inventions.

Elijah McCoy Travels to Scotland:

After Elijah turned fifteen, he left his home in Upper Canada. He went to Edinburgh, Scotland. Scotland is a part of the United Kingdom (UK) in Western Europe.

Elijah's parents worked hard to help their son. They saved enough money to send him to Scotland. His reason for going there was to become a mechanical engineer apprentice. Mechanical Engineering deals with how mechanics are applied. It deals with designing and operating machines.

MECHANICAL ENGINEERING DEALS WITH HOW MECHANICS ARE APPLIED AND WITH DESIGNING AND OPERATING MACHINES.

An apprentice is someone who is being trained and supervised by an expert. The expert trains the apprentice in return for work being done by the apprentice. Since the apprentice is being trained, he or she does not receive a lot of pay for the work.

Elijah's apprenticeship lasted for five years. After Elijah completed it, he was qualified as a master mechanic and engineer.

ELIJAH'S APPRENTICESHIP LASTED FOR FIVE YEARS.

Elijah Returns to North America:

Elijah returned to Upper Canada when his apprenticeship was over. Since he could not find a job, he decided to move. He headed to Ypsilanti, Michigan. He was twenty-two years of age at the time.

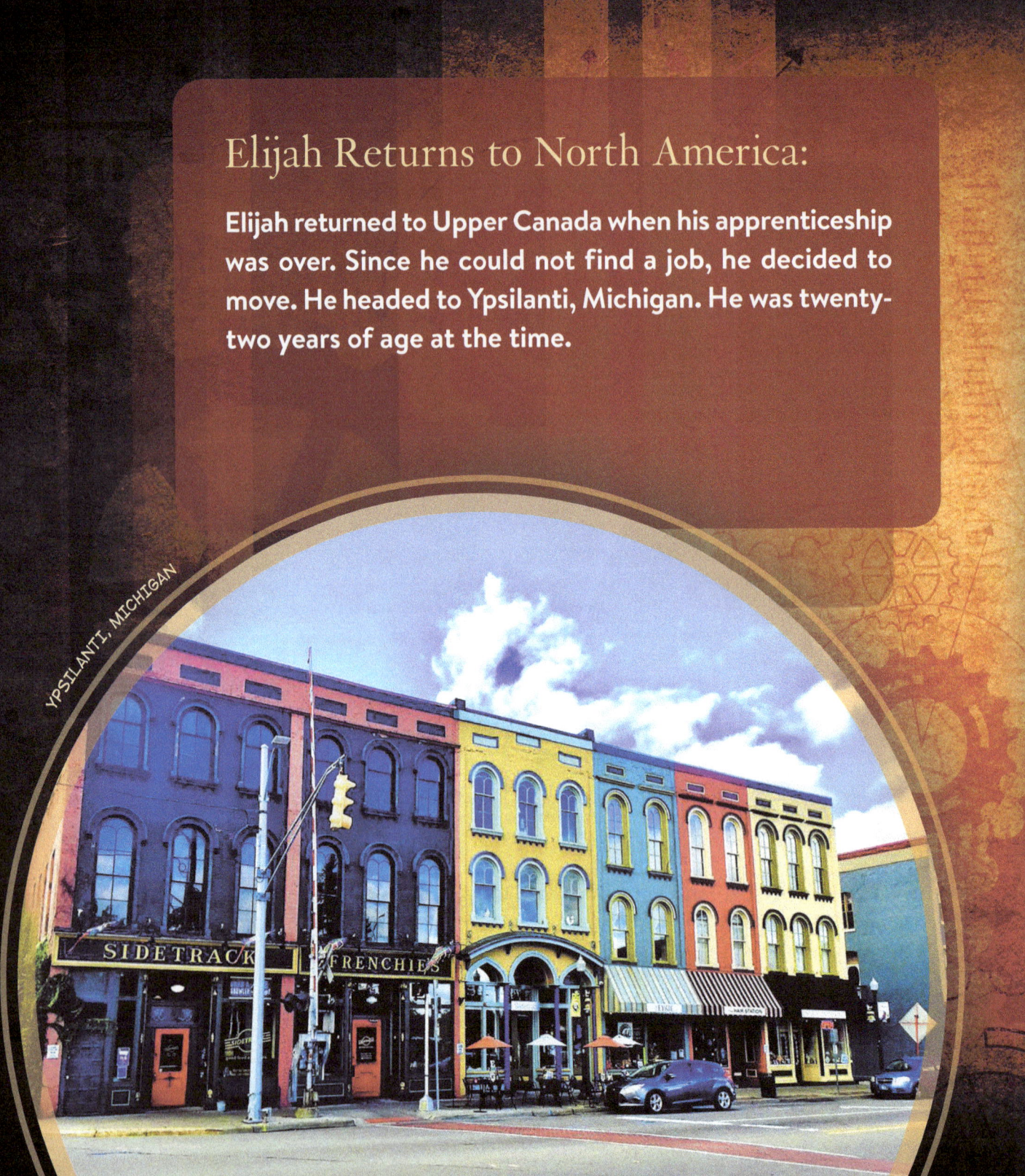

YPSILANTI, MICHIGAN

This was right after the American Civil War had come to an end.

THE AMERICAN CIVIL WAR WAS MOSTLY FOUGHT TO END SLAVERY.

Did you know?

The American Civil War was mostly fought to end slavery. It was from 1861 to 1865. Some states were free states. Others were slave states. The slave states refused to give up slavery even when it was against the law. For this reason, the free states and the slave states went to war. The free states won.

IN THE AMERICAN CIVIL WAR, THE FREE STATES AND THE SLAVE STATES WENT TO WAR.

Because of racism, he found it hard to find a job. Racism involves being unfair and unkind to someone only because of their race. Even though he was highly qualified as a mechanical engineer, he got a job as a fireman. It was at the Michigan Central Railroad.

RACISM INVOLVES BEING UNFAIR AND UNKIND TO SOMEONE ONLY BECAUSE OF THEIR RACE.

ELIJAH WAS RESPONSIBLE FOR SHOVELING COAL INTO THE TRAIN'S FIREBOX.

Some of his duties involved oiling the parts of the train that move. These included bearings and axles. They were oiled while the train was stopped. He was also responsible for shoveling coal into the train's firebox.

DETROIT, MICHIGAN

Elijah made his home in Detroit, Michigan in 1882. While there, he did work for different engineering companies. They would hire him for his expert advice on mechanical engineering.

Many years later, when Elijah was in his late seventies, he set up his own business. It was called the Elijah McCoy Manufacturing Company. He did this in 1920.

WHEN ELIJAH WAS IN HIS LATE SEVENTIES, HE SET UP HIS OWN BUSINESS

ELIJAH WAS MARRIED TWICE IN HIS LIFETIME.

Elijah's Marriages:

Elijah was married twice in his lifetime. The first marriage was to Ann Elizabeth Stewart. They got married in 1868. They had only been married for four years when she died. Elijah got married again. His second wife was Mary Eleanora Delaney. They would remain married for fifty years.

CHAPTER TWO:
The Inventions of Elijah McCoy

One of the most famous inventions that Elijah came up with was an automatic oil pump. He got the idea for it when he was working at the Michigan Central Railroad.

ELIJAH INVENTED AN AUTOMATIC OIL PUMP.

MICHIGAN CENTRAL STATION WAS THE MAIN INTERCITY PASSENGER RAIL DEPOT FOR DETROIT, MICHIGAN UNTIL THE HISTORIC LANDMARK WAS CLOSED DOWN AND ABANDONED.

Lubricating or oiling the parts of the train was dangerous work. When Elijah first started doing it, the work had to done by hand. Somebody had to then go to each of the parts that had to move. This job was done by holding a can of oil or lubricant.

WHEN ELIJAH FIRST STARTED LUBRICATING OR OILING THE PARTS OF THE TRAINS, THE WORK HAD TO BE DONE BY HAND.

ELIJAH'S JOB WAS DONE BY HOLDING A CAN OF OIL OR LUBRICANT TO THE PARTS THAT HAD TO MOVE.

ANY ENGINE THAT WAS POWERED BY STEAM WOULD HAVE MECHANICAL PROBLEMS FROM THE INDUSTRIAL OILS.

At this time, any engine that was powered by steam would have mechanical problems from the industrial oils. The problem was that the oils would not stay very long on the parts. As a result, the machines would overheat and become corroded. When something is corroded, it means that it is damaged or destroyed.

This happens to metals, stones, and other such materials. It is caused by a chemical action. A lot of fuel was wasted. Not only that but the trains would have to stop often. This was so that they could be oiled again. It was inconvenient and a waste of time. Elijah's automatic oil pump changed all this!

THE TRAINS WOULD HAVE TO STOP OFTEN SO THAT THEY COULD BE OILED AGAIN.

ELIJAH CAME UP WITH A METHOD OF OILING THE MOVING TRAIN PARTS WITHOUT THE NEED TO STOP ON THE TRACKS.

Elijah came up with a method of oiling the moving train parts. It was faster, better, and much less dangerous than how trains were being oiled at the time. There was no longer a need to stop on the tracks while a person went from one place to another oiling moving parts.

This invention was made after Elijah had been working for six years for the Michigan Central Railroad. Elijah would spend time at a machine shop that he had from his home. He kept working until he found a much better way for engines to be oiled.

ELIJAH KEPT WORKING UNTIL HE FOUND A MUCH BETTER WAY FOR ENGINES TO BE OILED.

He designed his automatic oil pump in a special way. It was so that the correct amount of lubricant could be given through a spigot. A spigot works like a faucet does.

A SPIGOT WORKS LIKE A FAUCET DOES.

E. McCOY.

Improvement in Lubricators for Steam-Engines.

No. 129,843.

Patented July 23, 1872.

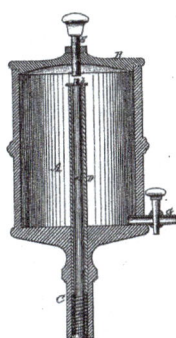

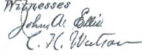

Witnesses
John A. Ellis
C. H. Watson

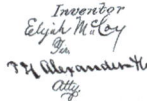

Inventor
Elijah McCoy
per
F. H. Alexander H.
Atty.

UNITED STATES PATENT OFFICE.

ELIJAH McCOY, OF YPSILANTI, MICHIGAN, ASSIGNOR TO HIMSELF AND S. C. HAMLIN, OF SAME PLACE.

IMPROVEMENT IN LUBRICATORS FOR STEAM-ENGINES.

Specification forming part of Letters Patent No. **129,843**, dated July 23, 1872.

SPECIFICATION.

To all whom it may concern:

Be it known that I, ELIJAH McCOY, of the city of Ypsilanti, in the county of Washtenaw and State of Michigan, have invented certain new and useful Improvements in Lubricators; and I do hereby declare that the following is a full, clear, and exact description thereof, reference being had to the accompanying drawing and to the letters of reference marked thereon, which form a part of this specification.

The nature of my invention consists in the construction and arrangement of a lubricator for steam-cylinders, as will be hereinafter more fully set forth.

In order to enable others skilled in the art to which my invention appertains to make and use the same, I will now proceed to describe its construction and operation, referring to the annexed drawing, in which is represented a longitudinal section.

A represents the oil-cup, provided with the cover B. In the center of the bottom of the cup A is a downward-projecting stem, C, to be screwed into the place where the lubricator is to be used. This stem is hollow, and from the same extends a tube, D, through the center of the cup. Within this tube is a rod, a, having a valve, b, at its upper end above the tube D to close the same, and at the lower end is a piston or disk, d, within the stem C. Around the lower end of the rod a, between the piston d and a shoulder in the stem, is placed a spiral spring, e, which forces the rod down, so that the valve b will close the upper end of the tube D and prevent the passage of the oil.

When the steam presses upon the piston the valve rises and allows the oil or other lubricating material used to pass out.

In the cover B is a thumb-screw, E, directly above the valve b, by means of which the flow of oil may be readily regulated. At the bottom of the oil-cup is a faucet, G, for the purpose of drawing off the condensed steam when necessary.

Having thus fully described my invention, what I claim as new, and desire to secure by Letters Patent, is—

1. The tube D, rod a, and spring e, in combination with the valve b and thumb-screw E and top B, the several parts being arranged to operate substantially as and for the purpose specified.

2. The stem C, tube D, rod a, and piston d, in combination with the spring e, when the spring is arranged in the stem and between the piston and end of the tube, substantially as and for the purpose set forth.

In testimony that I claim the foregoing as my own I hereby affix my signature in presence of two witnesses.

ELIJAH McCOY.

Witnesses:
S. M. CUTCHEON,
W. R. SAMSON.

Elijah received a patent for this invention in 1872. This is the same year in which it was invented. A patent is an official government certificate that gives rights to inventors. It gives the inventor the right to decide who can use his or her invention.

Did you know?

In addition to patents, there are trademarks and service marks. A trademark is a symbol, a word, or the like. It is used by one person or company for their products. When it is used to describe a service, it is called a service mark. Both are sometimes simply called marks.

A TRADEMARK IS A SYMBOL OR WORD THAT IS USED BY A PERSON OR COMPANY FOR THEIR PRODUCTS.

**DETROIT
LUBRICATOR
COMPANY**

"Genuine
Detroit"

In addition to making this invention, Elijah taught others how to use it properly. He worked with employees at the Detroit Lubricator Company. His work did not end there.

ELIJAH WORKED WITH EMPLOYEES AT THE
DETROIT LUBRICATOR COMPANY.

ELIJAH'S WORK WOULD END UP HAVING A LARGE IMPACT ON DIFFERENT MODES OF TRANSPORTATION IN THE 1800S.

He also kept on designing new devices for lubricating different mechanical engines. His work would end up having a large impact on different modes of transportation in the 1800s. They were able to operate more smoothly.

The automatic oil pump has also come to be called an oil drip cup. It became a success! In addition to being used on trains, it was used on steam ships, ocean liners, and factories that made machines.

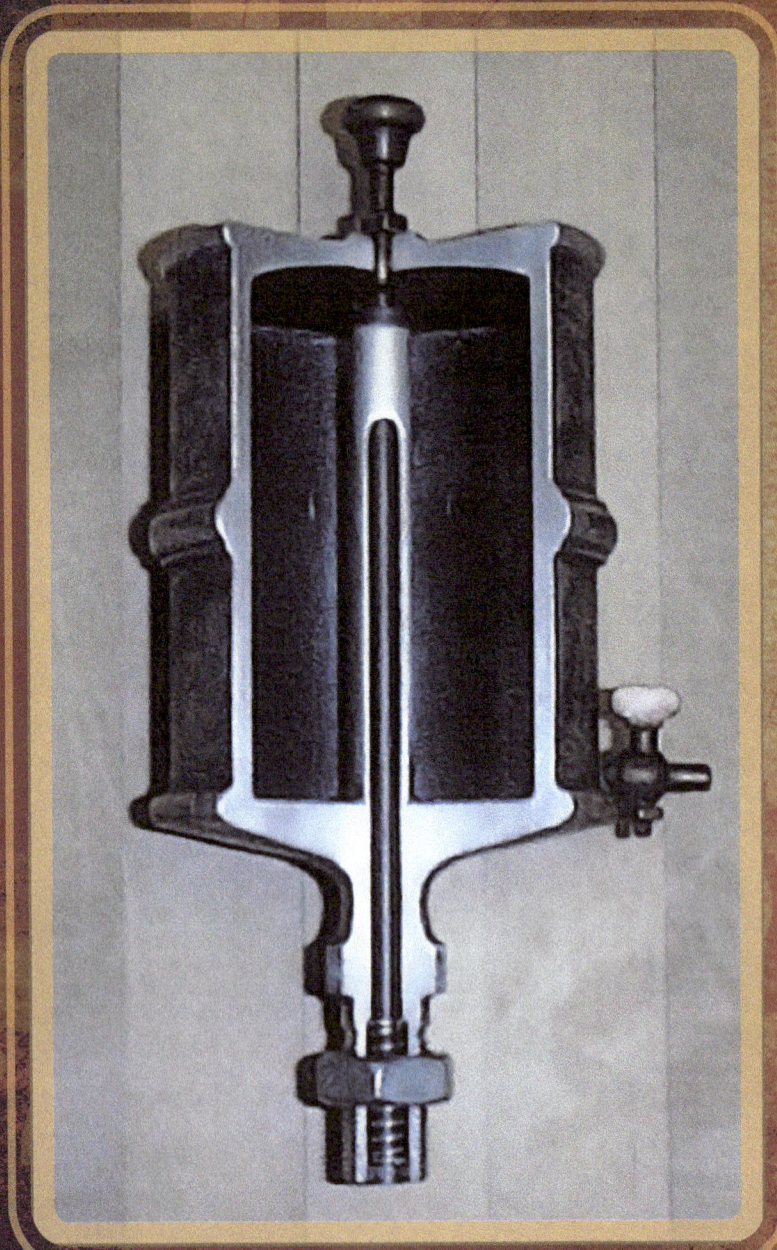

THE AUTOMATIC OIL PUMP HAS ALSO COME TO BE CALLED AN OIL DRIP CUP.

THE AUTOMATIC OIL PUMP
WAS USED ON STEAM SHIPS,
OCEAN LINERS, AND FACTORIES
THAT MADE MACHINES.

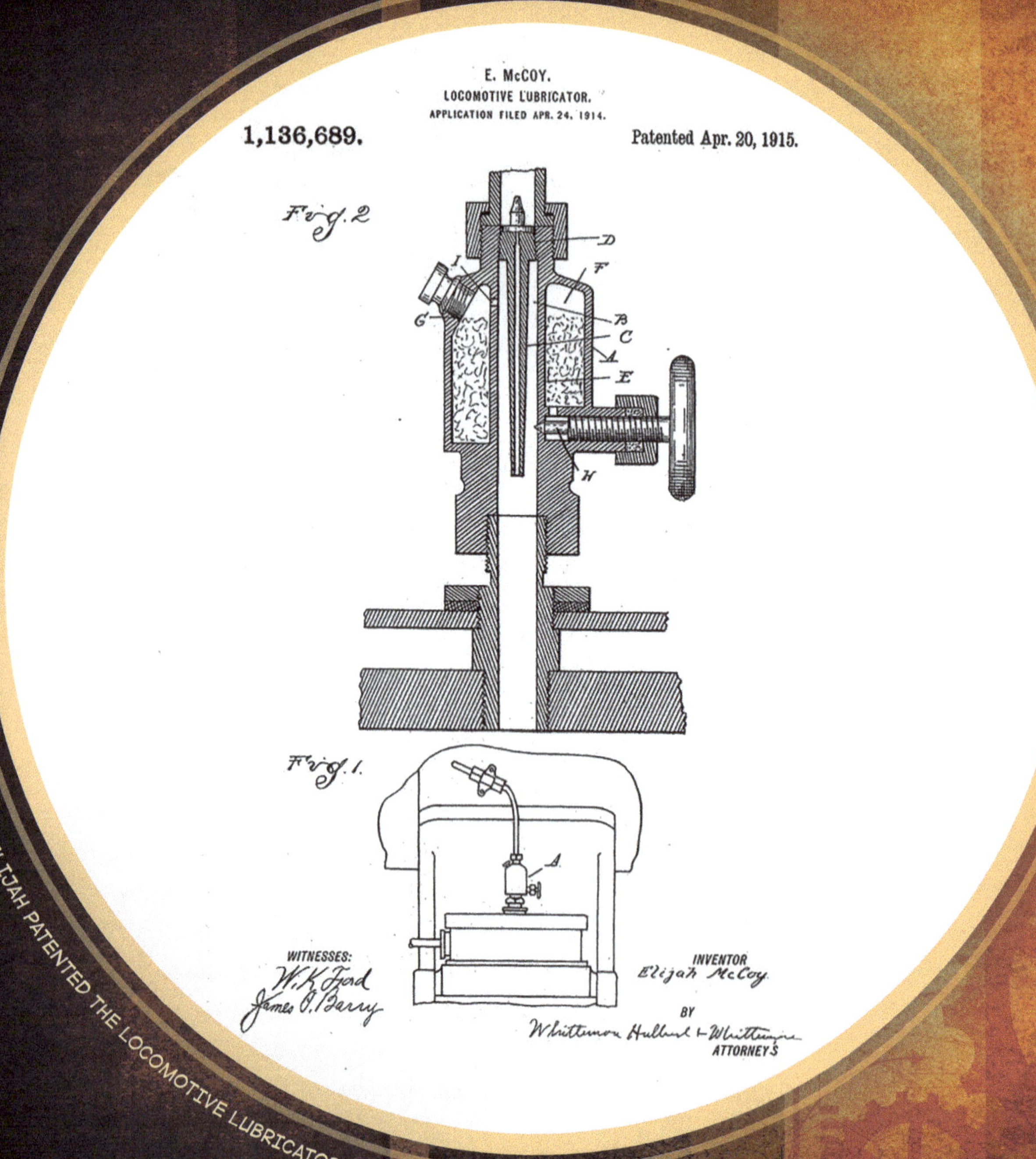

E. McCOY.
LOCOMOTIVE LUBRICATOR.
APPLICATION FILED APR. 24, 1914.

1,136,689.

Patented Apr. 20, 1915.

Fig. 2

Fig. 1

WITNESSES:
W. K. Ford
James P. Barry

INVENTOR
Elijah McCoy
BY
Whittimore Hulbert & Whittimore
ATTORNEYS

ELIJAH PATENTED THE LOCOMOTIVE LUBRICATOR IN 1915.

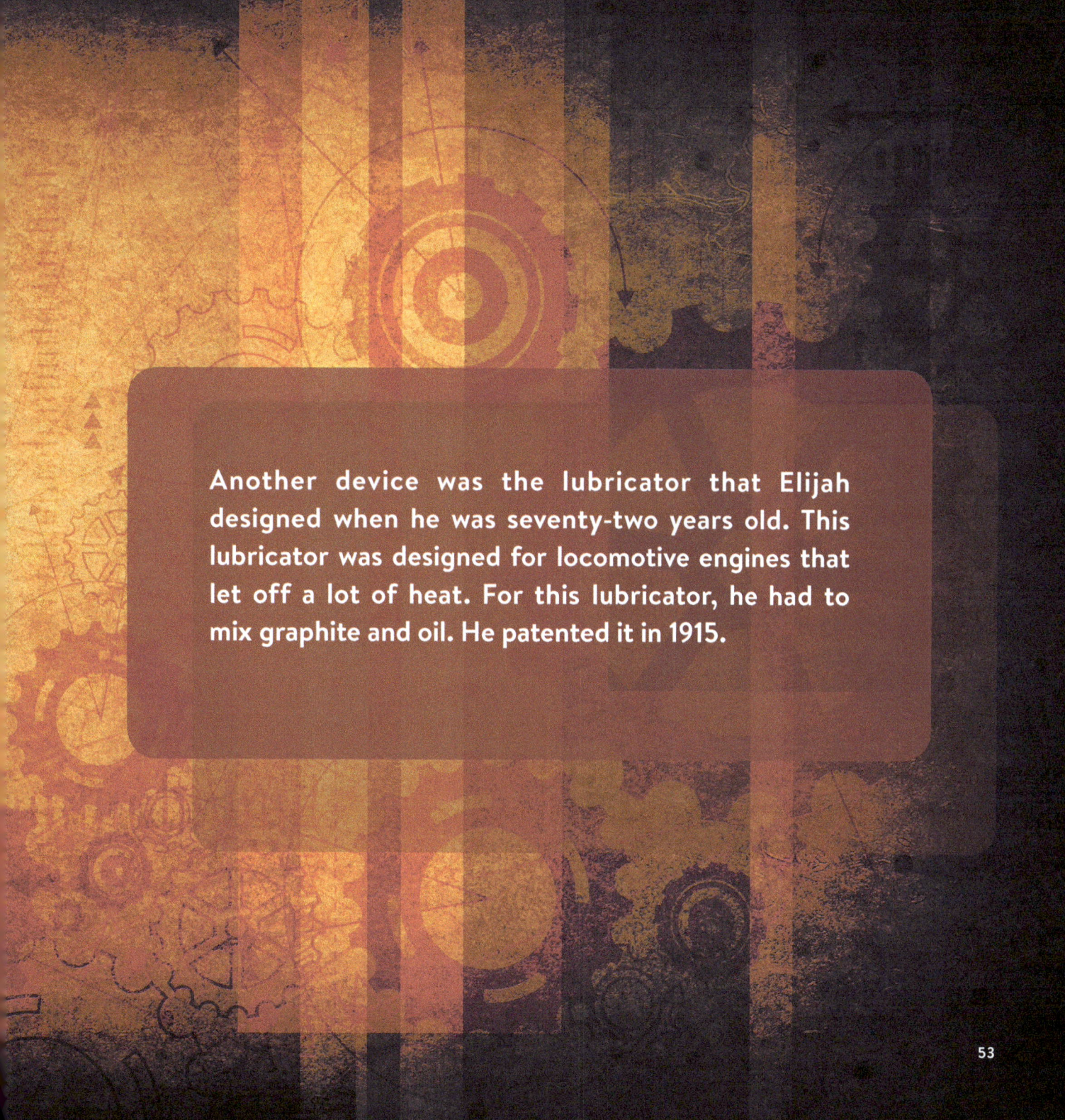

Another device was the lubricator that Elijah designed when he was seventy-two years old. This lubricator was designed for locomotive engines that let off a lot of heat. For this lubricator, he had to mix graphite and oil. He patented it in 1915.

Did you know?

Graphite is a type of pure carbon. It is a soft, slippery substance. Carbon itself is a chemical element of great importance. It is found in the crust of the Earth. Carbon can be combined with other natural elements. They form compounds. Graphite is one of two main types of carbon in its pure form. Diamond is the other.

GRAPHITE IS A TYPE OF PURE CARBON.

LAWN SPRINKLER SYSTEM

Almost all of Elijah's inventions were related to oiling machines. However, some were not. For example, he invented a lawn sprinkler system. He made improvements to rubber heels on footwear. He also came up with a portable ironing board.

ELIJAH MADE IMPROVEMENTS TO RUBBER HEELS ON FOOTWEAR.

PORTABLE IRONING BOARD

57

Elijah ended up with over fifty patents for his inventions. He was still working on inventions even in his late seventies. When he started his company in Detroit, the main reason was to produce his latest patented invention. It was an air-brake lubricator.

ELIJAH ENDED UP WITH OVER FIFTY PATENTS FOR HIS INVENTIONS.

Of all the inventions, Elijah is said to have felt that his automatic oil pump was the best.

CHAPTER THREE:
The Death and Legacy of Elijah McCoy

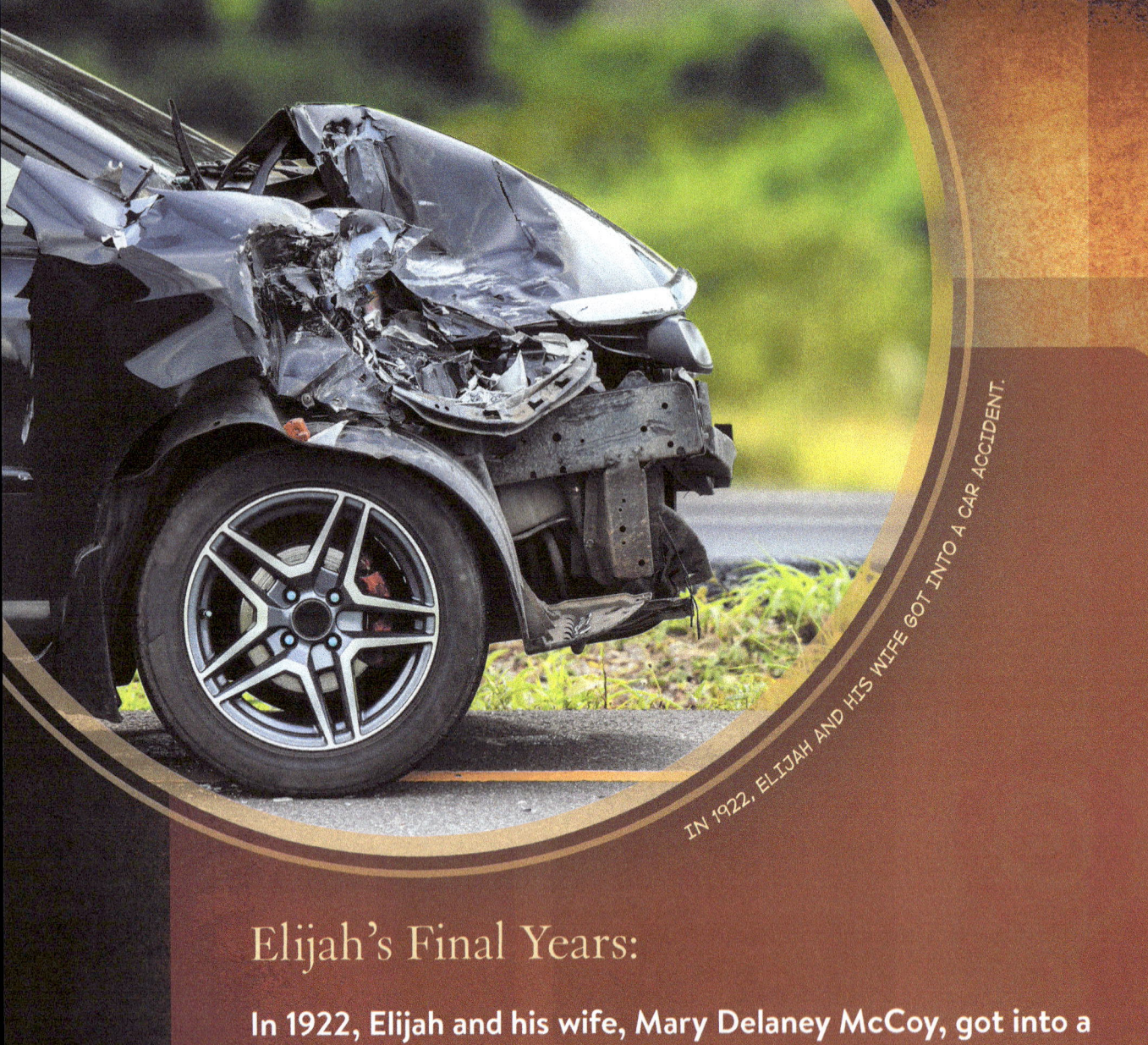

IN 1922, ELIJAH AND HIS WIFE GOT INTO A CAR ACCIDENT.

Elijah's Final Years:

In 1922, Elijah and his wife, Mary Delaney McCoy, got into a car accident. Both survived but Mary had different injuries. In 1923, she died as a result of them. Elijah's health started to get worse after the death of his wife.

He would spend the rest of his days in a state home. It was called the Eloise Infirmary. It was a place for those who did not have much money. After selling the rights to a lot of his patents, he ended up with little money. He remained at the infirmary until his death on October 10, 1929.

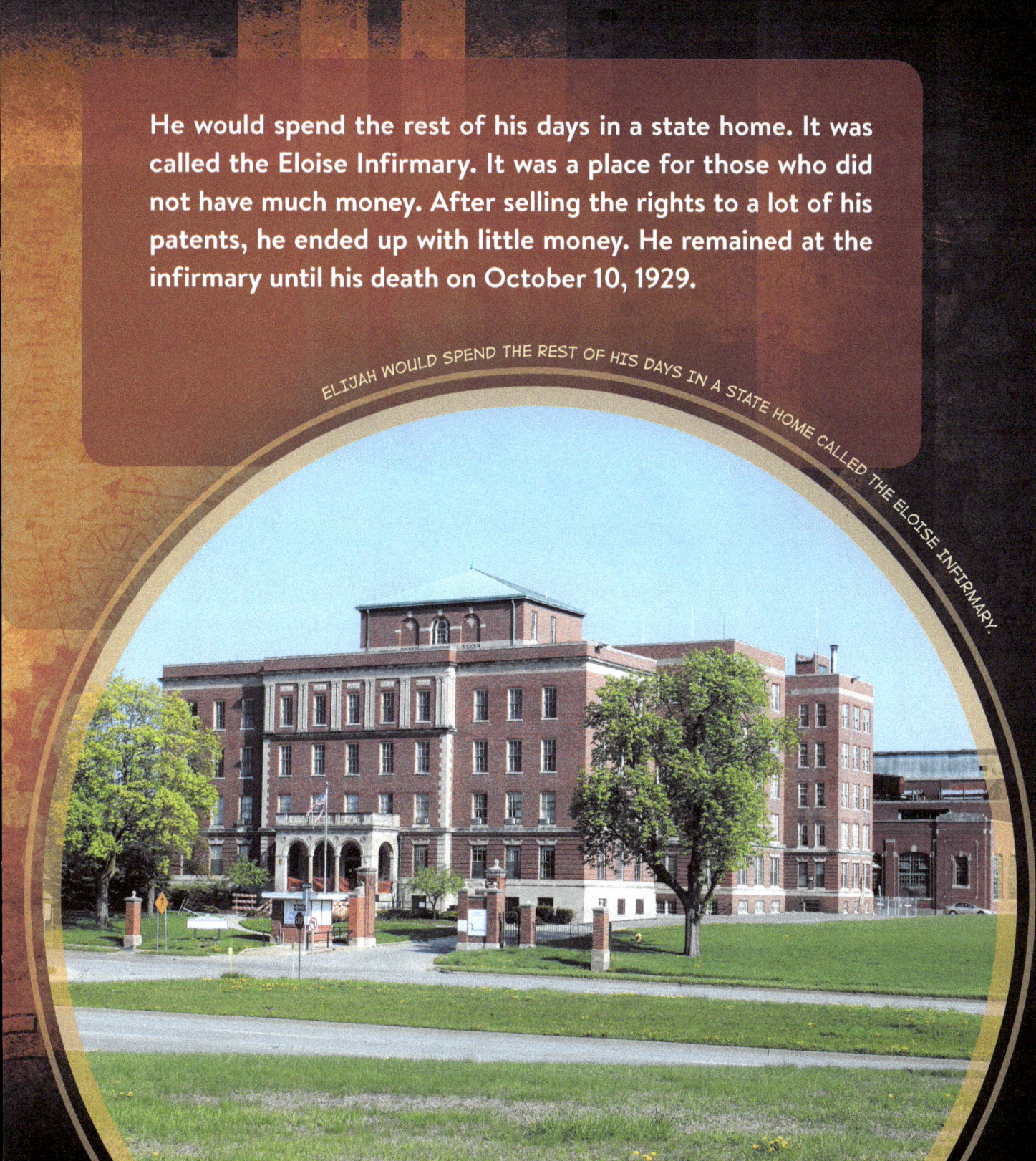

ELIJAH WOULD SPEND THE REST OF HIS DAYS IN A STATE HOME CALLED THE ELOISE INFIRMARY.

Elijah's Recognition and Legacy:

Elijah McCoy has been recognized and remembered since his death. It is said that Elijah was the African American to have received the most patents. This was at the time in history in which he lived.

ELIJAH WAS THE AFRICAN AMERICAN TO HAVE RECEIVED THE MOST PATENTS.

The expression, the real McCoy is said to describe Elijah's automatic oil pump. Nobody is exactly certain where the phrase came from. However, it seems to refer to people asking for Elijah's automatic oil pump instead of any other.

In 1974, a historical marker was put at the site of one of the homes in which Elijah lived. This was in the state of Michigan. There was also one put at his grave site. A year later, the city of Detroit called a street after him.

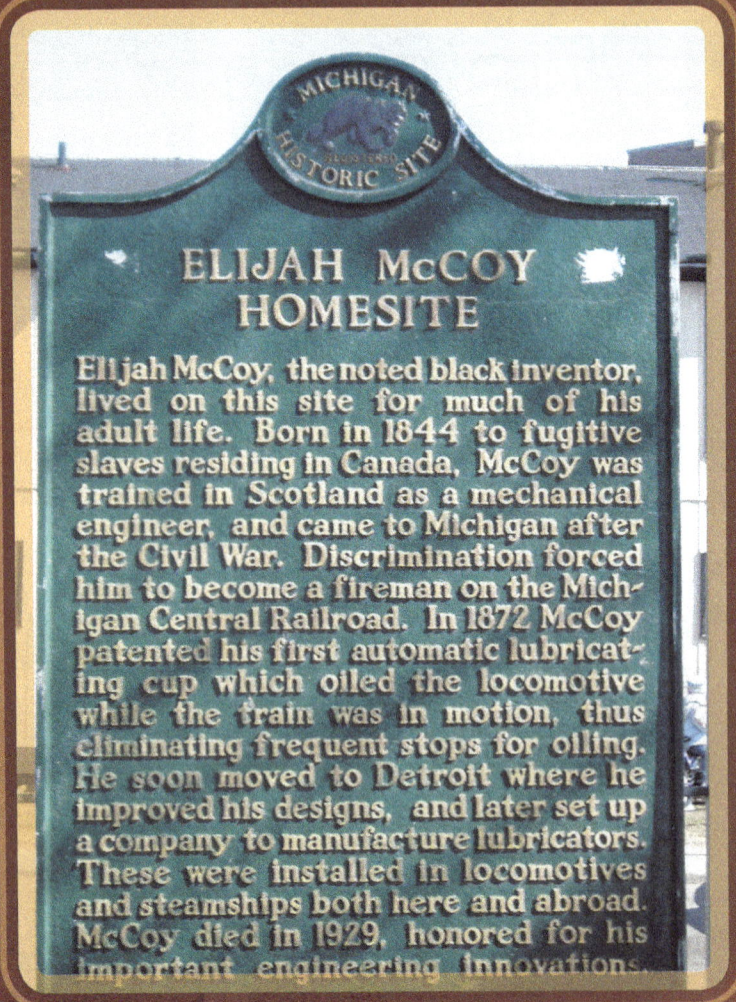

ELIJAH McCOY HOMESITE

Elijah McCoy, the noted black inventor, lived on this site for much of his adult life. Born in 1844 to fugitive slaves residing in Canada, McCoy was trained in Scotland as a mechanical engineer, and came to Michigan after the Civil War. Discrimination forced him to become a fireman on the Michigan Central Railroad. In 1872 McCoy patented his first automatic lubricating cup which oiled the locomotive while the train was in motion, thus eliminating frequent stops for oiling. He soon moved to Detroit where he improved his designs, and later set up a company to manufacture lubricators. These were installed in locomotives and steamships both here and abroad. McCoy died in 1929, honored for his important engineering innovations.

HISTORICAL MARKER AT THE SITE OF ONE OF THE HOMES IN WHICH ELIJAH LIVED IN MICHIGAN.

In 1994, a historical marker was put near the first workshop that he had. This was in Ypsilanti, Michigan.

In 2001, Elijah was included in the National Inventors Hall of Fame. This is in Alexandria, Virginia.

In 2012, the first satellite office of the United States Patent and Trademark Office was set up. It was in Detroit, and it was named after Elijah.

ELIJAH J. MCCOY MIDWEST REGIONAL OFFICE IN DETROIT, MICHIGAN.

Elijah McCoy was a talented man. He invented many useful things. One of the most well-known is the automatic oil pump. He invented other lubricators as well. In addition, he invented a lawn sprinkler system, and a portable ironing board. He also improved the rubber heels that were on shoes. Elijah was born in what is now Canada. He was born to African Americans who had fled there. They wanted to be free from being slaves. Elijah studied and became an apprentice in Scotland. He eventually ended up living in the United States. He would remain there until his death. For more biographies of famous people, look for other Baby Professor books!